Everything Donald Trump Knows About Australia

Making Books Great Again

by We The People

Tiny Hands Publishing
ISBN: 1-945674121
ISBN-13: 978-1945674129

DEDICATION

To the extensive team of researchers who worked tirelessly to assemble everything that Donald Trump knows about this subject.

Everything Donald Trump Knows About Australia

Everything Donald Trump Knows About Australia

Everything Donald Trump Knows About Australia

Everything Donald Trump Knows About Australia

Everything Donald Trump Knows About Australia

Everything Donald Trump Knows About Australia

Everything Donald Trump Knows About Australia

Everything Donald Trump Knows About Australia

Everything Donald Trump Knows About Australia

Everything Donald Trump Knows About Australia

Everything Donald Trump Knows About Australia

Everything Donald Trump Knows About Australia

Everything Donald Trump Knows About Australia

Everything Donald Trump Knows About Australia

Everything Donald Trump Knows About Australia

Everything Donald Trump Knows About Australia

Everything Donald Trump Knows About Australia

Everything Donald Trump Knows About Australia

ABOUT THE AUTHOR

We The People began writing on January 20, 2017 when the United States was temporarily seized by a delusional, cabbage-smelling tyrant with tiny hands that dwarfed his IQ. We The People will continue producing work that exposes the "vastlessness" of his knowledge until the country is reclaimed.

Yes, vastlessness is a word. It's a tremendous word. Believe me. Better than all those fake words.

www.ingramcontent.com/pod-product-compliance
Lightning Source LLC
Chambersburg PA
CBHW071646040426
42452CB00009B/1777
* 9 7 8 1 9 4 5 6 7 4 1 2 9 *